RATTLESNAKES

THE SNAKE DISCOVERY LIBRARY

Sherie Bargar   Linda Johnson

Photographer/Consultant: George Van Horn

Rourke Enterprises, Inc.
Vero Beach, Florida 32964

Library of Congress Cataloging in Publication Data

Bargar, Sherie, 1944-
  Rattlesnakes.

  (The Snake discovery library)
  Includes index.
  Summary: An introduction to the physical
characteristics, natural environment, and
relationship to human beings of the various species
of rattlesnakes.
  1. Rattlesnakes—Juvenile literature. [1. Rattle-
snakes. 2. Poisonous snakes. 3. Snakes] I. Johnson,
Linda, 1947-   . II. Van Horn, George, ill.
III. Title. IV. Series: Bargar, Sherie, 1944-
Snake discovery library.
QL666.069B39   1986   597.96   86-15467
ISBN 0-86592-956-4

Printed in the USA

Copy 3
4/02

Title Page Photo:
South American Rattlesnake
Crotalus durrisus terrificus

TABLE OF CONTENTS

RATTLESNAKES

All 70 kinds of **poisonous** rattlesnakes are a part of the *Crotalid* family. The unique hollow rattle on the rattlesnake's tail has no feeling. It is made of loosely connected parts of hard material like human fingernails. A new part of the rattle is added each time the snake sheds. The deaf snake cannot even hear the sound of its own rattle.

Eastern Diamondback Rattlesnake
Crotalus adamanteus

WHERE THEY LIVE

The deserts, mountains, woods, and swamps of the United States and Mexico are the homes of rattlesnakes. Some species are found in Central and South America.

The shy rattlesnake hides in cracks, in the **burrows** of other animals, and under bushes. These places keep it warm in the winter and cool in the summer.

Eastern Diamondback Rattlesnake
Crotalus adamanteus

HOW THEY LOOK

The heavy, strong bodies of rattlesnakes are different lengths. The pigmy rattlesnake is about 18 inches long, but the Eastern Diamondback Rattlesnake is about 5 feet long. The **keeled** scales of the rattlesnake make different patterns. Some have bands and others have diamond patterns on their backs.

*Dusky Pigmy Rattlesnake
on the back of a
Central American Rattlesnake*

*ose up of keeled scales of
ntern Diamondback Rattlesnake*

THEIR SENSES

The rattlesnake flicks out its tongue to pick up the scent of its **prey**. The Jacobson's organ in the roof of its mouth **analyzes** the scent to learn what is nearby. At close range, the eyes and heat receptor pits on the face of the snake give it the location and size of the **prey**. As soon as the **prey** is close enough, the rattlesnake strikes.

Eastern Diamondback Rattlesnake
Crotalus adamanteus

Mexican Pigmy Rattler Sistrurus ravus

Black-tailed Rattlesnake Crotalus molusus

THE HEAD AND MOUTH

The rattlesnake's wide triangular head has two heat receptor pits. Long, hollow fangs which are folded against the roof of the mouth are extended during a bite. Muscles around the **venom** glands pump the **venom** through the fangs into the **prey**. The jaws stretch like a rubber band to swallow the animal whole. The windpipe extends from the throat to the front of the mouth and allows the snake to breathe while swallowing **prey**.

Eastern Diamondback Rattlesnake
Crotalus adamanteus

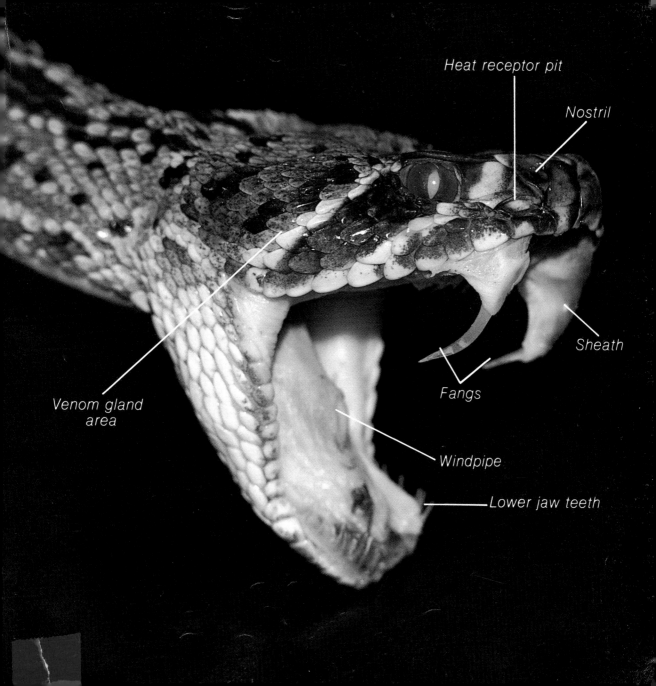

Heat receptor pit

Nostril

Sheath

Fangs

Venom gland
area

Windpipe

Lower jaw teeth

BABY RATTLESNAKES

All species of rattlesnakes differ slightly, but in late summer or early fall the Eastern Diamondback Rattlesnake has 10 to 15 babies. The babies are about 12 inches long and weigh about 3 ounces. The newborn snakes take care of themselves immediately. Within one year the Eastern Diamondback Rattlesnake may be 3 feet long and weigh as much as 4 pounds.

Juvenile Eastern
Diamondback Rattlesnake

PREY

The rattlesnake skin provides **camouflage** in its habitat. Hidden from view, the rattlesnake relies on surprise as the key to successful hunting. Mice, rats, birds, and lizards are its usual prey, but a large rattlesnake can swallow a 5 pound rabbit. The rattlesnake injects its **venom** and waits for the **prey** to die. Then the prey is swallowed whole.

Eastern Diamondback Rattlesnake
Crotalus adamanteus

THEIR DEFENSES

Camouflage protects the rattlesnake from its enemies. Unable to hide, a rattlesnake will flee from danger. When it cannot get away from an enemy, it puts its body in a coil, faces its enemy, and shakes its rattle to let others know it is there. The sound of the rattle can be heard 100 feet away. If the enemy moves too close, the snake strikes.

Albino Western Diamondback Rattlesnake
Crotalus atrox

RATTLESNAKES AND PEOPLE

Rattlesnakes eat rats and mice which destroy farmer's crops. Scientists are studying the rattlesnake **venom** to learn more about the human body. The biggest enemy of the rattlesnake is people because they are destroying the rattlesnakes' natural habitats.

GLOSSARY

analyze (AN a lyze) analyzes — To find out what something is.

burrow (BUR row) — A hole dug in the ground by an animal for its home.

camouflage (CAM ou flage) — The color of an animal's skin matches the color of the ground around it.

keeled (KEEL ed) — Having a ridge down the middle.

poison (POI son) poisonous — A substance that causes sickness or death when it enters the body.

prey (PREY) — An animal hunted or killed by another animal for food.

venom (VEN om) — A chemical made in animals that makes other animals and people sick or kills them.

INDEX